the Full Monty

Handbook

A Buzz Book
St. Martin's Press
New York

Book Design/Layout: David Everitt

Web Site: http://www.buzzmag.com
Web Site: http://www.foxsearchlight.com

ISBN 0-312-18345-3

First Buzz Book Edition: August 1997

10 9 8 7 6 5 4

Letter from the Editor

The Full Monty is all about men who dare to bare, and in this special edition of *The Full Monty Handbook*, we're taking you along for the ride.

But The Full Monty doesn't start and stop with a skin show—it dares to bare far more than male flesh. The Full Monty bares men's souls: It's a peep show of the male ego. Body image, desirability, and youth are no longer issues that plague only women. These days, a bad hair day, a flat ass, a tight stomach, or a chest that defies gravity—even legs shaved smooth without nicks or cuts—are all of equal concern among the sexes. Face it, men ain't what they used to be, and for a lot of women that's really terrific news. But for many—especially men—this recent shift in male identity has created mass confusion.

Over the past ten years, men have been sexualized and objectified in the media just as mercilessly as the gals, and don't think it hasn't had an impact. Seven men open up and bare their love handles in a no-hold-barred chat about their bodies and what they'd change if they had a magic wand. Their answers might surprise you.

Remember when male strippers were as novel as designer jeans and microwave ovens? It's been nearly twenty-five years since the Chippendales dancers first took the stage—sporting nothing but satin G-strings and bow ties—creating a dramatic shift in the way women related to men as a form of entertainment. Over the past three decades, a whole lot has happened to the genre of male exotic dancing; and for a quick run down of the highlights you may want to peruse our list charting the ever-changing aesthetics, trends, and fashions of the male striptease since it's birth in the late 1970s.

Have you got what it takes to take it off? You may be surprised. Check out The Full Monty Quiz For Men and find out. And if you ace our quiz, you'll surely be in need of our male stripping How To Guide. And who knows, you just might be in store for a bright, new career.

If you're a dirty dancing dude at heart, but think that a spare tire, a beer gut, or a pair of broomstick legs stands between you and a successful career dancing nude at bachelorette parties, we've got good news: there's just the right dance for your body type, and we'll tell you what it is. If you're not ready to go The Full Monty just yet—and opt for a G-string or a bikini brief—we'll show you how to play down your body flaws and enhance your god-given gifts—all without going to the gym.

Do you know the difference between a widger and a bugger? How about a hump and a shag? As you'll discover, The Full Monty men have their own inimitable way of communicating with one another, and if you have any trouble following their conversations you might want to consult our slang dictionary. Remember, knowledge is power.

So peel down to your skimpiest bikini brief and slather yourself with body oil, because here we go...

And we're going The Full Monty.

Ta,

Eds.

TABLE OF CONTENTS

THE FULL MONTY

MEN

WHO ARE THEY?

FIVE WOMEN SHOOT FROM THE HIP AND CALL 'EM AS THEY SEE 'EM.

We asked:

Loretta, 35, landscape designer
Carla, 32, mother
Jill, 24, graduate student
Maxine, 46, art director
Maryjean, 38, piano teacher

And here's what they said:

GAZ

The gang's roguish cheerleader, Garry (a.k.a. Gaz), is constantly trying to get the show off the ground and keep the guys together. It's no easy task, especially when he's told by his ex-wife that he can't see his son, Nathan, because he can't pay child support. With nothing to lose, Gaz decides that The Full Monty may be the answer to get him off the dole and earning a few dollars. But, will he be able to keep the men together and have the guts to show his widger in public?

Maryjean: UGH! I've known a hundred guys like that! Even if he had a steady job he'd do something to mess it up and get himself fired. Gaz is one of those guys that gets fired from every job he's ever had, but always blames his boss, or some guy at work; it's never his fault. He's always broke, even when he's working.

Jill: Deep down I think Garry's a good person, he probably had a screwed up childhood. You can tell that he loves his son deeply—his son is the center of his universe.

Loretta: Garry's a terrible role model for his son; he's setting an awful example. Nathan (his son) is going to be totally screwed up. I'd hate to hear what a therapist would say to him.

Carla: He's a LOSER! If he spent half as much time looking for work as he did hanging out with his friends, he'd be able to make those child support payments. There's no focus in his life; he's a bit of a flake. I bet he never shows up on time for anything.

WHAT MOTIVATES GAZ TO TAKE IT OFF?

Maryjean: Easy money. He has no concept of what it is to hold down a job.

Carla: I think he seriously believes he's god's gift to women. He thinks he's really hot, and wants to show off. He obviously needs attention, that's why he's such a jerk and is always making a fool of himself and picking fights. He's *way* jealous of the Chippendales dancers.

Loretta: I think Garry *loves* the idea of having a bunch of women watch him on a stage dancing naked—he was way too eager to get the group together. He used those child support payments as a guise. He probably wanted to go full monty all along, but never had the nerve to say so.

Jill: I really believe his son (Nathan) was his motivation—but I think Garry would do anything for a buck.

DAVE

Too overweight to even sneak through the window of the bathroom at the nightclub, Dave is convinced his marriage is failing because of his chubby body. But, he can't seem to find the willpower to lose it. He half-heartedly joins the troop at Gaz's urging, but still thinks that people will laugh him off the stage. He convinces himself that The Full Monty is a bunch of malarky and that they will all make asses out of themselves. Will Gaz be able to convince him that it's worth a buck or two to strip? Or will it be someone else?

Loretta: I think Dave is the only member of the group that really understands what women go through trying to live up to unrealistic standards of beauty and what it's like to be judged solely on your appearance. He's the only one that really learned anything from his stripping experience.

Carla: Dave's whole world has been turned upside down, and he's caught in between playing it safe and taking risks.

Jill: Dave is extremely sensitive and introspective. I'm sure he never had erectile dysfunction before he lost his job; the battle with his weight and the stress of losing work is just too much for him.

Maxine: Like with his eating, Dave struggles with choosing what he has to do and choosing what he wants to do.

Loretta: Dave takes life way too seriously. He likes to sabotage himself.

WHAT MOTIVATES DAVE TO TAKE IT OFF?

Carla: The money had something to do with it, but for Dave I think it was all about overcoming personal obstacles: his weight, his closet-eating, his impotence, his shyness, his own masculinity. I think Dave *had* to do it—for his own sake.

Jill: I think Dave wanted to prove to himself that he could get up there and not get laughed off the stage.

Maryjean: Dave needed to feel attractive to women, and he wanted to be able to break loose like that. But he needed the added incentive of money and the support of other men who look as bad as he does to help him do it.

GERALD

Seen as an old fool by the other men, Gerald has been unemployed and at the Job Club for six months, but still hasn't found a way to tell his spend-happy wife about their financial straights. His skill as a dancer drives the fellows to seek his help, but it's Gerald's desperation and his own drive to perform that convinces him to go along with the Full Monty enterprise. Despite having a fit now and then, Gerald does a pretty good job as choreographer and manages to whip the boys into a regular bunch of Chippendales. But, when he gets a job on the day of the performance, will he still want to whisk off his clothes in public?

Carla: Gerald is a major control freak. Even when his life is falling apart, he still puts on a suit and tie and pretends like everything is just fine. That's very alcoholic behavior. He probably had alcoholic parents.

Maryjean: Did you see the way he grabbed the video remote from the police officer? That says it all.

Loretta: Gerald internalizes everything. He probably has ulcers.

Jill: I think Gerald needed his reality shaken up a little bit; he needed Garry and the others to loosen him up. I think the whole experience was a major turning point in Gerald's life. He's probably never let himself go like that.

Maxine: He let himself go, but he did it in a very Gerald sort of way; it was all very controlled: the dance steps, the timing, the rehearsals. Gerald could have never just jumped up on a table and gone The Full Monty; he had to have choreographed moves and weeks of rehearsals. Gerald has probably never had a spontaneous moment in his life. He's probably a lousy lay.

WHAT MOTIVATES GERALD TO TAKE IT OFF?

Loretta: I think he got off on the control of being choreographer and telling everyone what to do. That's also why he was fore-man at the steel mill. That's the only way he can feel powerful in life, telling other people what to do—he has no power at home.

Carla: Gerald was desperate to keep up appearances; it was the money.

Maxine: I think this was Gerald's way of coping with a mid-life crisis. Dancing naked in front of women makes him feel youth-ful and desirable again.

Maryjean: The only reason he went through with it is because Gerald needs to finish everything he starts; he's very anal.

LOMPER

Lomper is the only member of the troop who has a job, which is ironic since he's such a stooge. You would think he'd be uptight over doing The Full Monty, being that he is skinny as a rail. But, Lomper becomes an entirely new person with the troop and even finds someone who can make him a little less of an oddball.

Carla: He gives me the creeps; he has weird eyes, you never really know what's going on in his head. He seems like he's always on the edge somehow. He's probably a sociopath.

Jill: I feel sorry for him. He's probably still a virgin.

Maxine: I think it's very interesting that of all the musical instruments, he chose a bugle; it's a phallic symbol.

Maryjean: He's an extremely lonely person to begin with; he has no friends except his invalid mother, plus he has to deal with feelings of alienation and decide about his sexuality—no wonder he's suicidal!

Loretta: Lomper's emotional development got stunted; he never matured emotionally. He's probably been under his mother's thumb his whole life.

Jill: He has a cute butt.

WHAT MOTIVATES LOMPER TO TAKE IT OFF?

Loretta: The feeling of belonging. It's very important to Lomper that he be included in a group—without his bugle.

Maryjean: I think that after Guy joined the group, Lomper stuck around so he could see Guy in a G-string, like he was getting away with something.

Jill: He wanted to do something daring and dangerous because he's always played it safe.

Carla: I think Lomper could be talked into doing anything; he's just so desperate for the companionship.

HORSE

"Old Geezer" Horse is afraid that his willy won't live up to his nickname when it's time to bare it all. Despite his age, he's the best dancer the troop has to offer. And, any guy who can move like Horse doesn't have to worry about having the guts to do The Full Monty.

Maxine: Horse is mysterious. He has secrets. Who knows what his story is.

Maryjean: Horse loves attention from women; he'd get up and dance with or without his pants. He just loves an audience.

Carla: Everyone keeps remarking how "old" Horse is, but I don't think he sees himself that way. In many ways, he has the most youthful spirit in the group.

Jill: Horse is the most normal one.

Loretta: If he can invite his family to watch their dress rehearsal, he must be cool. Horse is very comfortable with who he is.

Carla: He's the only one with any talent.

WHAT MOTIVATES HORSE TO TAKE IT OFF?

Jill: I think he just wanted to have fun with it.

Loretta: It was kind of a big joke for Horse; he wasn't ashamed or embarrassed; he probably invited his whole family.

Maryjean: A good time—Horse is the kind of guy that clears a dance floor, he's always the life of the party.

Carla: He liked the idea of dancing for an audience, but I really don't think he wanted to go all the way. A G-string was cool with him, but for Horse, I think going all the way took some of the fun out of it and made it vulgar. I think he felt they had crossed some kind of line with that.

Maxine: It was an outlet for his wild side.

GUY

Guy is a free spirit with whale size tackle and can't wait to strip down to nothing in public. A bit of a kook, Guy seeks out new adventures with boundless enthusiasm but not much brains. For Guy, The Full Monty is a brilliant way to show the world that his lunchbox is most definitely full. But, will he be serving the girls or the guys?

Maryjean: I'll bet Guy has a sordid past.
Carla: He's cute.
Loretta: I think he sleeps around—men, women, all the action he can get.
Maryjean: Guy's the type that has two sets of friends. One set of nice friends who think he's straight, and another set of wild friends that he parties and goes barhopping with.
Jill: I think he's a decent person; he seems caring.
Maxine: He has the kind of self confidence that can only come from being well-hung.

WHAT MOTIVATES GUY TO TAKE IT OFF?

Maryjean: He loves showing off his tubesteak.

Carla: He knows he's the hottest one in the group, and likes upstaging the others and being the center of attention.

Loretta: I think he totally gets off on having an audience. He's obviously worked hard for those stomach muscles and probably takes his shirt off every chance he gets.

Maxine: Guy's a total exhibitionist. He probably likes to be watched which is why he jumped at the opportunity to strip.

Jill: He's doing it for the attention; he already has a job.

Maryjean: He's totally on his own trip; he seems very detached from the rest of the group. For Guy, it's all about Guy.

CONFESSIONS

OF THE FULL MONTY MEN

Stripping down to your Y-fronts is no easy business unless your idea of fun is getting laughed out of town by everyone you know. Just ask the boys who've been there—Gaz, Gerald, Dave, Horse, Guy, and Lomper. They've gone The Full Monty. But they didn't get the idea on a whim and it wasn't only for the money. Each of the boys had a really good reason for taking their clothes off. But easy it wasn't.

DAVE:
"I try dieting; I do try. Feels like I've been on a diet all me life. The less I eat, the fatter I bloody get. It's not meant to work like that is it? I was even using the cling-film bit. How was I supposed to take a bloody stage and take me kit off when I can't even get down to it with me own wife?

I'm not a bloke who's cut out for showing his widger in public. Who's gonna wanna see a fat tosser like me go The Full Monty. I bloody prayed the lasses are understanding about us. What if four hundred of 'em showed up and said, 'He's too fat,' 'He's too thin,' and 'He's a pigeon-chested little bugger.'"

GUY:
"Always wanted to be a dancer. Me favorite film's "Singin' in the Rain" where they do that walking up wall thing...bloody ace, it is. Plus for strippin' I've got me lunchbox."

HORSE:
"Never really saw myself as a pro, but I had the moves: The Bump, The Stomp, The Bus Stop, The Funky Chicken,...my break dancin days are over. It's been a while, mind. And I've got a dodgy hip. When I heard about the stripper auditions, I thought it'd be a reet easy way to earn a few quid. And they needed me too, those blokes pranced around like they were having a bleedin' eppy.

"Problem is, I told 'em me nickname was Horse, figurin' I'd never have to prove it. See, me bollocks do a fine job of fillin' me kegs, but the willy has shrunk with the years a bit. But then bog-eyes (Gaz) comes up with the divvy notion of goin' The Full Monty. So what am I gonna do? Me widger isn't tiny, but I ain't no farm animal neither."

GAZ:
"The lasses were there to watch them Chippendales poofters—baying or blood. Ten quid an' all to watch some poof get his kit off! Ten quid! I figure it was worth a thought. I got to get some brass together to pay Mandy the bloody maintenance if I want to see me son, Nate. Can't make much in a factory or such, so I reck what the heck—we'd do those Chippendales woofters one better, we'll give those lasses The Full Monty."

LOMPER:
"Eight hundred quid I needed to buy me mum a chair lift—saves me carrying her up and down the stairs five times a day. No problem takin' off me kit for that. But The Full Monty—knickers and all— hell-fire!"

GERALD:
"An irritating bunch of chuffers them were, Gaz and Dave. I was on the dole going on six months, get the first job interview I've 'ad in a reet long while—and those two buggers show up and ruin it for me. It damn near gave me an eppy.

"Gaz says stripping! Oh yeah, I'm thinking, can just see Little and Large prancin' around Sheffield with their widgers hangin' out— widgers on parade, bring your own microscope. I told them flat out, 'You're both fucking ugly.' I tell 'em, dancers have coordination, skill, timing, fitness, and grace—take a reet hard look in the mirror!

"I do dance quite well you know. But blimey—a professional like me can't very well go on in public with me willy hanging out. It's not my kind of dancin'—it's all arse-wigglin'—but straight up, I had a bloody good time of it!"

DO *YOU* HAVE WHAT IT TAKES TO TAKE IT OFF?????

TAKE THE FULL MONTY QUIZ AND FIND OUT

As we approach the next millennium, men find themselves redefining manhood: They're reinventing their roles in the home, in relationships, and in the workplace. The old, rigid standards that once dictated the limits of masculinity and manliness have come down like the Berlin Wall. We live in an age of stay-at-home-dads, the "men's movement," and the "sensitive guy." Rock stars are hitting the golf course, tattooed Gen X studs are painting their toenails and wearing eye makeup, and men who once knocked themselves out in a gym five days a week in a fervid effort to get *ripped*, now hit the yoga mat for a kinder, gentler, *inner* workout.

Men now have more paths to choose from than ever before; they're able to create themselves as they see fit, rather than squeeze themselves to fit a hampering pre-fab mold. And all things being equal, male strippers can follow suit. If the man of the house no longer need be the primary breadwinner, why does a male stripper have to have washboard abs? The guys who dream of taking it off in front of an enthusiastic throng of horny women need not ascribe to the Chippendales standards of the 70s and 80s. What once had to be tight, tanned, and topped with a can of hairspray is now open to interpretation—and might take a different form entirely. Just because you've got a bit of a paunch and hair on your back, or boney knees and a flat ass, or prefer "The Hustle" to a back flip doesn't mean that you too can't stuff it into a G-string and bump 'n grind with the best of them. An unabashed dirty dancing dude with a sense of humor, and at least one good move, can make just as many bills as the pro if he knows how to work his audience.

For each of the following questions, circle only one answer that best applies to you:

#1. If I had to rate myself as a dancer I'd say:
a) I could easily make the final cut on MTV's The Grind.
b) I wouldn't win any contests.
c) I'm a shitty dancer, but my enthusiasm makes up for my lack of ability.
d) I can do a mean Macarena.
e) I'd rather watch Soul Train.

#2. If I had to rate my body, I'd say:
a) Compared to me, Brad Pitt looks like Fred Mertz.
b) I look pretty decent in a swimsuit.
c) I'm three hundred pounds of pure fun!
d) My body is beginning to sag in places it never did before and it frightens me.
d) I'm seriously considering lipo, and avoid mirrors at all costs.

#3. I am comfortable naked...:

a) As long as I have a good tan and the pimples on my back hav
   cleared up.
b) Only in front of my spouse, or in front of men who have smalle
   penises than me.
c) Anywhere—I am an unadulterated exhibitionist.
d) As long as those present are naked too.
e) Only in the dark.

#4. My butt:

a) Defies gravity.
b) Has been referred to as "cute."
c) Is as white as a paper plate in a snowstorm.
d) Is two-thirds of my body weight.
e) Is as flat as a tennis court and nearly just as wide.

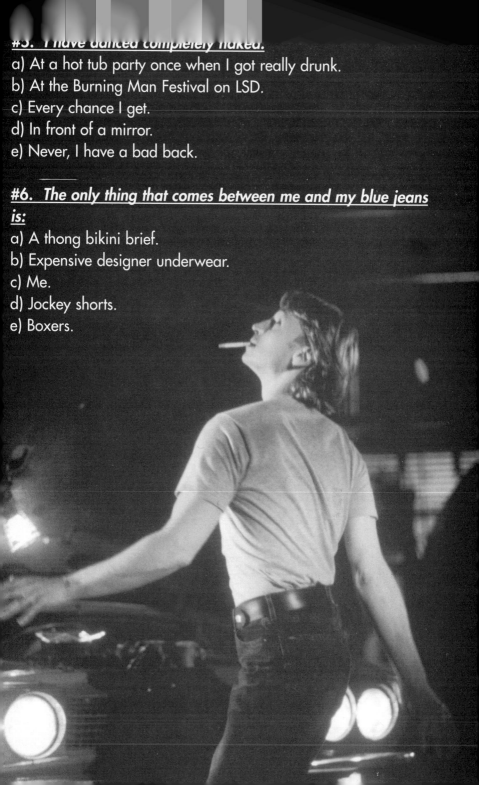

#5. I have danced completely naked.
a) At a hot tub party once when I got really drunk.
b) At the Burning Man Festival on LSD.
c) Every chance I get.
d) In front of a mirror.
e) Never, I have a bad back.

_____

#6. The only thing that comes between me and my blue jeans is:
a) A thong bikini brief.
b) Expensive designer underwear.
c) Me.
d) Jockey shorts.
e) Boxers.

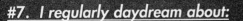

#7. I regularly daydream about:
a) The Barbi Twins.
b) Sharon Stone.
c) Rosie O'Donnell.
d) Cindy Crawford.
e) Anna Nicole Smith.

#8. My hair is:
a) Loaded down with lot of hair care products.
b) Cut and styled at a trendy salon.
c) An unruly mass of cowlicks.
d) Falling out.
e) A weave.

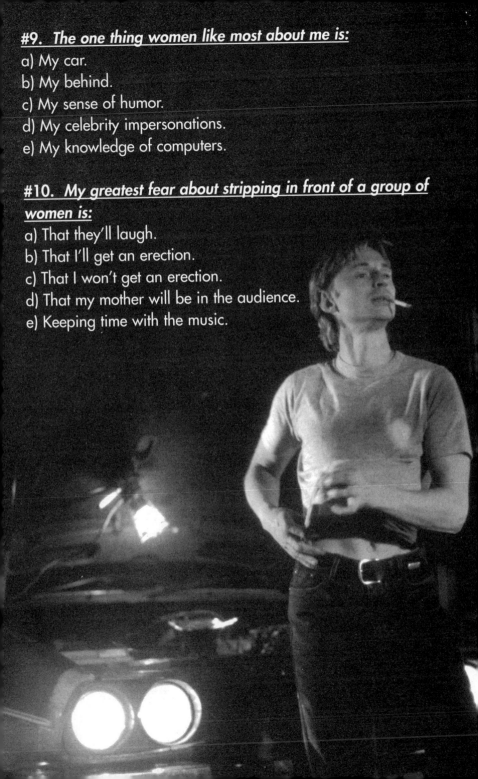

#9. *The one thing women like most about me is:*

a) My car.
b) My behind.
c) My sense of humor.
d) My celebrity impersonations.
e) My knowledge of computers.

#10. *My greatest fear about stripping in front of a group of women is:*

a) That they'll laugh.
b) That I'll get an erection.
c) That I won't get an erection.
d) That my mother will be in the audience.
e) Keeping time with the music.

#11. *When I go to the beach I generally wear*
a) A Speedo.
b) Loose fitting surfer jams.
c) Nothing—I only go to nude beaches.
d) Something high-waisted.
e) A wide brimmed hat and lots of sunblock.

#12. *I freely disclose my sexual fantasies:*
a) To anyone who'll listen.
b) On the second date.
c) Only if I'm asked.
d) To a phone sex operator.
e) To my psychiatrist.

#13. *I have privately fantasized about:*
a) Switching places with Tommy Lee.
b) Being a porn star.
c) Dancing nude at a bachelorette party.
d) Food.
e) Paying off my credit card debt.

How did you rate??

Give yourself 8 points for answer a, 4 points for answer b,
16 points for answer c, 2 points for answer d,
and 0 points for answer e.

Scoring:

*192-208: Shake your money maker! Invest in a good G-string;
you're headed toward a bright future!*

*104-192: You show tremendous potential—work on your
hamstring stretches.*

*52-104: Practice, practice, practice. (Have you considered a
career as a medical assistant?)*

26-52: Don't quit your day job.

0-26: Do not pass GO, do not collect $200.00.

POURING HOT STEEL INTO A THONG BIKINI MIGHT SPELL TROUBLE:

Whatever your body type, there's a G-string that's just right for you.

From the way you fit into a satin G-string, it would seem that god never intended for you to work a catwalk with ten dollar bills folded into your waistband and squealing women pawing at your behind.

Does spandex gather and bunch in all the wrong places? Does a thin elastic waistband only enhance your love handles? Does your pouch slouch?

You may simply need to come to terms with your body type, and take our crash course in exotic dancewear. Make no mistake: You too can undress to impress—and look your best while you're doing it!

THE MICHELIN MAN

The upside to being a Michelin Man is that you're not alone. Nearly every adult male that has ever walked planet earth knows what it is to hit 35 and Pow!: The metabolism slows down, and the skin that once slid comfortably into the waistband of your trousers now hangs over your pockets like unbaked cookie dough. The really painful question to ask yourself is whether you're a One-Tire, Two-Tire, or Three-Tire Michelin Man (For those exceeding three tires please see The Watermelon.). The Michelin Man needs **vertical lines** to take the eye up and down, rather than side to side (your love handles will do that just fine on their own). Your best bet is a cod piece/harness combo. These contraptions are usually fashioned out of black leather and are a bit on the S&M side (which isn't such a bad thing; think props). The thin, horizontal waistband won't draw too much attention to the excess flesh jiggling above each of your hips, and the V-shaped front pouch extends into medium-width shoulder straps that draw the eye up, adding some width throughout the shoulders and chest, helping to balance your thick midriff. You can easily unsnap and unzip the harness to tease and please—all the while playing down your spare tire.

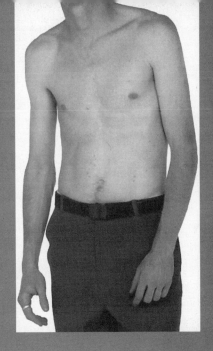

THE WISHBONE

On one hand, god was good to you. He gave you a high metabolism that allows you to wolf down the food that The Michelin Man and The Watermelon only dream about. On the other hand, during lovemaking women may complain about your razor-sharp hip bones or your dagger-like elbows. For you we have two words: *horizontal lines*. You want to create the illusion of width in the upper thighs and draw attention away from your protruding hips. This can be accomplished with a skin-tight, low-riding brief cut straight across the top of the legs (May we suggest wet jockey shorts?). If you're eager to show a little more skin and have your sight set on a thong brief, make sure that the V-shape of the front pouch is extra wide, and attached to a hefty waistband. In fact, you might want to go with real undergear in lieu of a G-string—it'll give you that jock-in-a-locker-room look that some women really dig!

THE REFRIGERATOR

You're a husky, sturdy, big-boned guy. You're probably clumsy too. All your body parts pretty much look the same: Some folks would be hard-pressed to tell the difference between one of your legs and one of your arms. Your neck is as thick as your waist, and your ankles and wrists are interchangeable. Face it, you're just plain big all over. Your problem is easily remedied however. You simply need to **create curves and contours**, and the easiest way to do this is with the classic bikini brief. The V-shaped patch of fabric above the buns will give a look of roundness to your big, flat, square behind. The front pouch will push your talent up and forward, giving some bounce to your well-grounded frame. You want to stay away from dark colors like black or navy, as they will work against you. Choose a bright color in a shiny fabric like spandex, or lurex with glittery threads; the reflected light will enhance those convex lines!

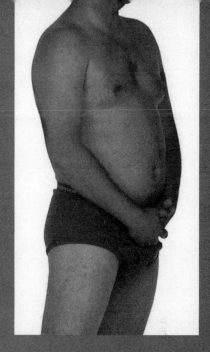

THE WATERMELON

You're a tough customer. You're big *and* round and this is not an easy thing to conceal. Sometimes life offers no simple solution, and for this reason we think it's best for The Watermelon to *play up* his size rather than try to mask it. Wear the tiniest, shiniest (sequins preferably) G-string that money can buy, with an elastic waistband so thin that it disappears into your fleshy folds. The effect of a seemingly free-floating patch of glitz holding your goods in place beneath a cement-truck like gut might pleasantly surprise you! Try a big jewel in your navel if you dare—you are someone who has nothing to lose!

THE BIRTH OF

THE MALE

STRIP

Before the advent of Chippendales, "girl's night out" didn't include men in satin G-strings. In fact, the only gals lucky enough to cop a peek at a near-nude male shaking his behind for cash to the tunes of Donna Summer were the fun-lovin' fag-hags who accompanied their homosexual pals to urban-area gay bars featuring live go-go boys.

It was back in the sexually liberated swingin' 70s when a soon-to-be notorious Hollywood club opened up—with a stringently enforced "women only" policy at the door. Soon the success of Chippendales would spread like wildfire; and new clubs popped up in several major cities throughout the U.S. The success of the Chippendales formula would also spawn innumerable copycat clubs anxious to cash in on the success of this new *for-women-only* entertainment trend.

Overnight, Chippendales became a household word—not so much as the name of a nightclub, but as a catch-all term for a very particular kind of *champagne-and-limos* male aesthetic. The Chippendales man always stood at least six feet tall, was unduly muscled, and eternally tanned. Never did he have a hair out of place or a blemish on his skin. These were Stepford Studs; your wish was their command. The main objective for a Chippendales dancer was to provide women with an object of desire, and to create an illusion of availability at the same time. And like the girls-next-door image of *Playboy Magazine*, the Chippendales dancers were good boys—not gigolos—quick to tell audiences while making the rounds on the talk show circuit that they were "working their way through college," or that stripping "helps to keep me in shape."

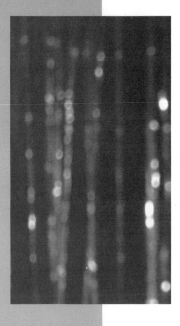

As well, lest anyone get the wrong impression from a group of men who use more hair products than Loni Anderson, spend all day in a gym, wear spandex, sequins and satin, smear their mouths with lip gloss, and keep a standing weekly appointment at the nearest tanning salon, they were all—each and every one of them—*heterosexual.*

At Chippendales, something is always left to the imagination—they never take it all off. But unfortunately for Chippendales, we live in a very unimaginative time. The ultra-liberated female strip club goers of the 90s would rather ogle an Italian Stallion swinging his meat within arm's reach, over watching the micro-basket of a Chippendales clone bounce nonthreateningly in a chorus line. And like the Playboy Club before them, Chippendales soon began to lose speed and vanish from the American landscape. Today, the name Chippendales means marketing more than anything else: videos, calendars, mugs, greeting cards, even underwear for men.

So where did the men of Chippendales go? They've gone legit — graduating from nightclubs to theaters — and taking their show on the road. These days, the production value of a Chippendale's Revue rivals that of a Broadway vehicle like *Miss Saigon* or *Les Mis*, only with lots of male T&A. Five or six dozen Chippendales clones pile on to the stage in fully choreographed song and dance numbers, featuring three-story high sets *and* completely nude dudes—either with their back to the audience or with the aid of a strategically placed hand prop, always leaving their audience wanting more.

Even in the 90s, they're still good boys.

STRIPPING

FOR YOUR MATE:

A "How-To" Guide

So what if she may have already seen you naked hundreds of times—she's never seen you naked *like this*. There's a big difference between standing in front of the bathroom mirror *sans* pants with your face slathered with shaving cream, and a rough, buff, down and dirty no-holds-barred lap dance right in the middle of your living room.

In order for this to work, you've got to be well-rehearsed. You'll also need to prepare your partner for the unexpected; create a mood for the exciting and the unpredictable. And it certainly doesn't hurt to ply her with alcohol or some other type of judgement inhibitor beforehand.

Important things to remember: Tease her for as long as you possibly can, but don't overdo it and lose your audience in the process; everything is better in moderation and timing is essential. Put her under your spell. Withhold body contact as long as possible. Work her into a lather. Make her *beg* for your flesh. Most importantly, make sure YOU clean up the mess of g-strings, props, jock straps, socks, shoes, splattered towels, or whatever else may be littering the floor after you've finished. Nothing kills the afterglow of a good striptease more than having to tidy up after the dancer, so don't stick her with that job.

THE COSTUMED STRIP

The Costumed Strip is to male stripping what the pie-in-the-face is to vaudeville: It's old shtick but it still works. There are a lot of gals who get weak in the knees over a man in uniform, so don't rule this one out!

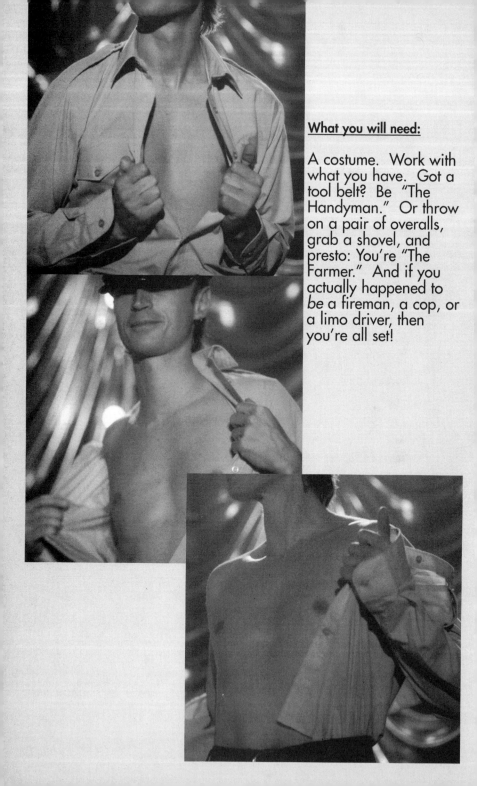

What you will need:

A costume. Work with what you have. Got a tool belt? Be "The Handyman." Or throw on a pair of overalls, grab a shovel, and presto: You're "The Farmer." And if you actually happened to *be* a fireman, a cop, or a limo driver, then you're all set!

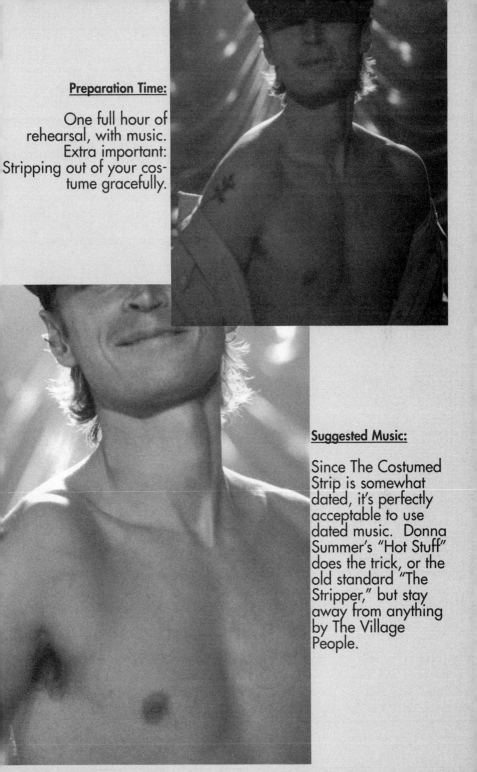

Preparation Time:

One full hour of rehearsal, with music. Extra important: Stripping out of your costume gracefully.

Suggested Music:

Since The Costumed Strip is somewhat dated, it's perfectly acceptable to use dated music. Donna Summer's "Hot Stuff" does the trick, or the old standard "The Stripper," but stay away from anything by The Village People.

THE BAD BOY STRIP

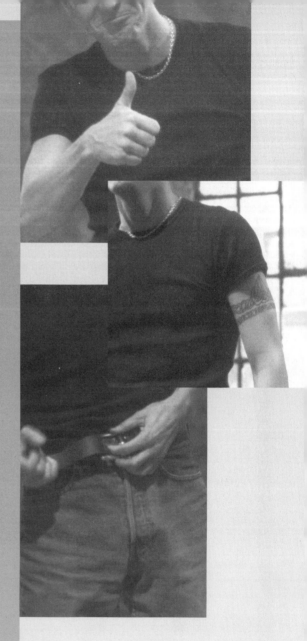

Only for the adventurous and truly uninhibited. This is a strip that could involve lots of hands-on interplay between you and your audience. Both of you should abstain from sex for at least a week prior to The Bad Boy Strip.

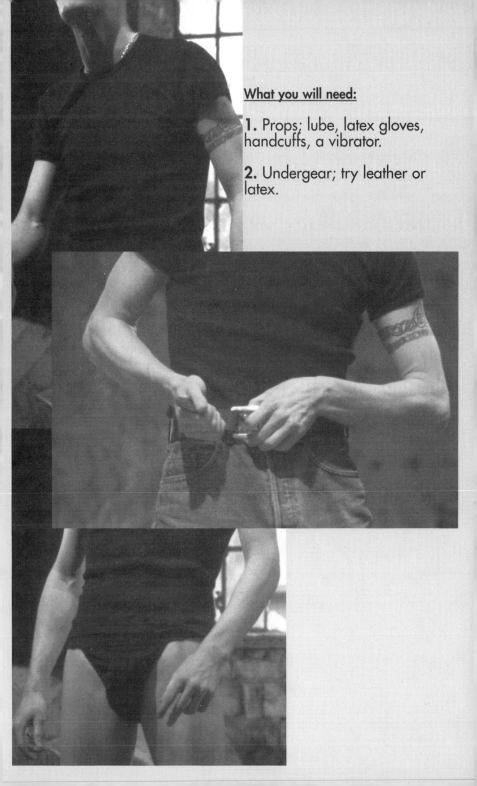

What you will need:

1. Props; lube, latex gloves, handcuffs, a vibrator.

2. Undergear; try leather or latex.

Preparation Time:

Several days. Take some time to think about this beforehand. What nasty things can your perverted little mind come up with? Take some time to practice privately with your props. Make sure the handcuffs are well oiled and won't jam. Check to make sure the vibrator has fresh batteries.

Movement:

The Bad Boy Strip is a no-holds-barred thang. If she's always wanted you to "perform" just for her, here's your chance to really wow her! It's perfectly acceptable to begin your act with a standard strip, but be sure your big finish consists of something that you've only done in the privacy of a dark bedroom.

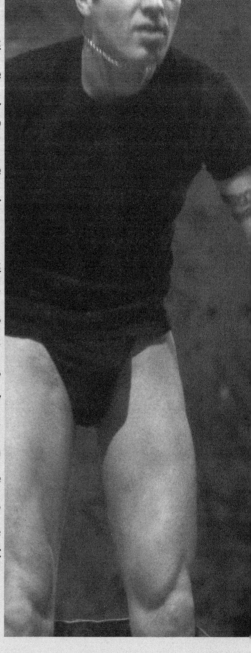

Suggested Music:

The Bad Boy Strip can last for hours. Extended-play techno works well (no vocal), or hard-hitting rap (as long as the lyrics focus on sex and not mayhem). Try "Sex On Wheels" by The Thrill Kill Cult, or almost anything by The Cramps.

THE MESSY STRIP

Male strippers love slathering themselves with messy stuff. They're especially big on baby oil. Whip cream is popular too, as is chocolate syrup. But the possibilities don't end there, be creative; barbecue sauce, hollandaise, even marinara might work. Do keep in mind that The Messy Strip is far more effective when your spouse is *hungry*. Instead of dinner, serve her *yourself* one night this week!

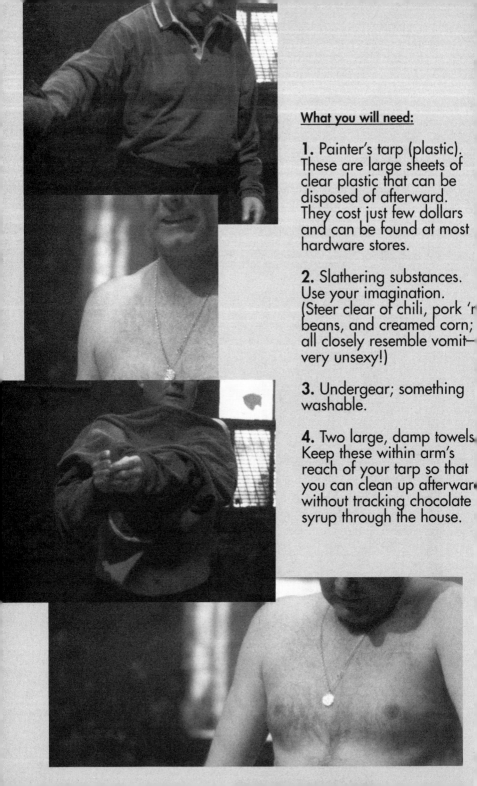

What you will need:

1. Painter's tarp (plastic). These are large sheets of clear plastic that can be disposed of afterward. They cost just few dollars and can be found at most hardware stores.

2. Slathering substances. Use your imagination. (Steer clear of chili, pork 'n beans, and creamed corn; all closely resemble vomit— very unsexy!)

3. Undergear; something washable.

4. Two large, damp towels. Keep these within arm's reach of your tarp so that you can clean up afterward without tracking chocolate syrup through the house.

Preparation Time:

ou should practice dancing for at least one full hour in front of a mir-
r, with music. Keep in mind that an authentic homemade marinara
uce needs a full day to cook properly. Hollandaise can be made from
powdered mix in less than fifteen minutes.

Movement:

eep your moves slow and steady, or you'll have slop flying all over the
om. Writhing on all fours, slow stretching, and forward bends com-
iment The Messy Strip. Keep in mind that a plastic sheet covered with
hipped cream can get awfully slippery; so watch your footing!

Suggested Music:

Having a song end in the middle of a dance is death to a
stripper! The Messy Strip takes some time, so make sure
you've got plenty of music; a full-length CD of extended-
play techno works well for The Messy Strip. Slow-and-
sexy jazz instrumentals are also very effective.

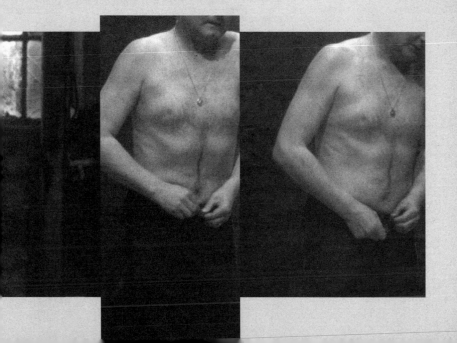

STRIPPING

DANGERS!!

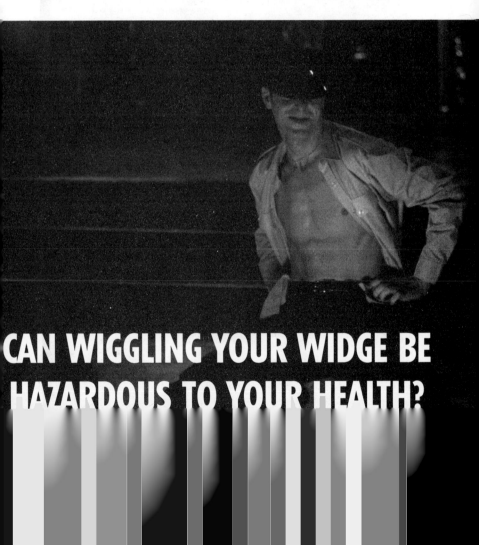

CAN WIGGLING YOUR WIDGE BE HAZARDOUS TO YOUR HEALTH?

While a star-jump, a low pelvic grind, or a back flip might look easy when performed on a spot lit cabaret stage by a seasoned male exotic dancer, those same moves performed by an uncoordinated amateur who doesn't know what the hell he's doing could produce long-term damage to the neck, hips, and spine. Know the risks before you shake those hips:

The Move: *Low pelvic grinding.* Common among strippers and easily executed by a flexible amateur, but beware: This move can spell trouble if you're not careful.

The Injuries: If you hyper-extend the lower back while you're grinding, you can cause a sprain, a spasm, or a herniated disk. By over-rotating the hips with an enthusiastic grind, it's possible that you may pop the ball joint out of the hip socket—which is not as dangerous as it sounds, but uncomfortable and something to be avoided nonetheless. You may also run the risk of pulling a hip flexor and/or groin muscle.

The Move: *Complete forward bend with straight knees.* This is a classic move for taking down the bikini brief to reveal a smaller G-string underneath. Every male stripper worth his weight in spandex has done this one.

The Injuries: Unless you have very flexible hamstrings—uncommon among men—this could mean one thing: Charlie Horse.

The Move: *Star-jump.* This is a flying leap in a spread eagle position, as though your entire body is forming a big "X."

The Injuries: Similar to the injuries produced by a botched low pelvic grind, the emphasis is placed on the hip flexors and the lower back. Also, a hard landing without considerable give in the knees could produce shin splints, where the muscle, running down the front of the shin from the knee to the ankle, rips away from the shin bone.

The Move: *A forward slide landing on bent knee.* An effective and dramatic move for a stripper, but murder on the knees if poorly executed.
The Injuries: Trauma to the knees. At best, knee injuries are slow to heal. At worst, might require surgery and may produce complications that last the rest of your life.

The Move: *Back flip.* An advanced move certainly, but if you've got these down you're sure to be bumped from the chorus line to the featured act.
The Injuries: If botched in a bad way; total paralyses. If you fall flat on your back, you're looking at a spinal fracture or complete break. Land on your neck instead of your hands, and you may cause damage to the vertebrae from the base of the head to the bottom of the neck. Another bad fall may bruise the tail bone—which is not only painful, but would have you bedridden until healed. Over rotate the flip, and your worst case scenario might be a broken rib and a punctured lung. A broken collar bone is another possibility. A rough landing on the hands might cause torn ligaments or sprained wrists.

The Move: *Upper body twisting.* An effective move with the performers naked back to the audience.
The Injuries: Overextended twisting could cause the intercostal muscles—the muscles between the ribs—to cramp. This is what's referred to as a "stitch."

The Move: *Back bends, or back bend variations.* Another common move for professional male exotic dancers; an old standard.
The Injuries: Shoulder dislocation, sprained hands or wrists, or harm to the lower back.

The Move: *Head thrashing.* A favored move for male strippers with long, rock 'n' roll hair; whipping the head back and forth.
The Injuries: This can easily strain the muscles in the neck. The injuries may not be apparent until the next morning when you can barely lift your head off your pillow. Excessive head thrashing could also pinch a nerve, completely immobilizing the neck for days.

---

aside from costly E.R. bills, attempting these moves without the proper training could lead to a badly botched routine. Nothing can kill the mood of a fervid exotic dance like bodily injury, plus you can end up looking like a complete ass. Worse, a fractured spine, a dislocated shoulder, or a broken collar bone is *very unsexy.*

SNAKE CHARMING

(KEEPING IT IN THE BASKET)

There's nothing like spontaneous arousal to spoil the lines of a well-fitted G-string. There you are one minute, bumping and grinding, and working up a sweat, with your talent snugly tucked into a satin pouch securely held in place by a couple of reliable elastic straps. The next minute, POW! From out of nowhere—almost as though it's got a mind of it's own—that unruly serpent begins to rear it's nasty head, straining at the leash in a fervent attempt to make it's surprise appearance. And since G-strings rarely give you room to grow, your encore might precede your big finish—leaving nothing to the imagination and killing your well-rehearsed tease.

So what are you supposed to do when your "dance partner" decides to work in a little choreography of it's own? While no method is foolproof, mind over matter seems to be your best bet when the unexpected arises; concentrate really hard on something super-gross, then, cross your fingers and knock wood.

Is the mind MIGHTIER than the sword?

Here's our top ten list of sure-fire, performance-tested erection killers:

(Clip this list and keep it in your pocket—
you never know when you might need it!)

1. Your grandmother naked
2. Open heart surgery
3. A dead puppy crawling with maggots
4. Drinking someone's vomit
5. Getting your eyeballs slashed with razor blades
6. Sucking on Donald Trump's toes
7. A sex-change operation
8. A catheter
9. A cat's butt
10. Michael Jackson's nose

MALE STRIPPING THROUGH THREE DECADES

Just as Compact Discs have replaced the LP,
microwaves have upstaged the conventional oven, and e-mail has made our postal workers look like a bunch of overpaid, gun-crazy morons, male stripping too has grown and changed over the years. What was born in the late seventies with the Chippendales chain evolved over the eighties and reached new extremes in the nineties. The archetypal stud costumes, ubiquitous throughout the infancy of male stripping, seem laughable by the standards of today. What once seemed tantalizing is now ridiculous. The "cops," the "cowboys," and the "construction workers" that graced the strobe-lit stages of yesteryear smack of the Village People or an Alan Carr production as we approach the next millennium.

Let's take a look back and examine how the aesthetics, styles, and trends of male stripping has transformed over the past three decades.

THE 70s	THE 80s	THE 90s
Hairspray	Styling Mousse	Extensions
Dollar Bills	Five Dollar Bills	Ten Dollar Bills
Sequins	Spandex	Rubber
Ass of Steel	Arms of Steel	Abs of Steel
Hairy Chests	Shaved Chests	Waxed Chests
A Tan	Tan Lines	Tattoos
The Gold Chain	A Diamond Stud in the Left Earlobe	Pierced Nipples
Imagination	Mesh	Cock Ring
White Men	Black Men	Latin Men
Cowboy Boots	Construction Boots	Doc Martens
A Breakaway Tuxedo	Jeans with Strategic Rips	A Leather Harness
A Top Hat & Cane	A Bull Whip	A Bottle of Lube
The "Bun Shake"	The "Floor Hump"	The "Lap Grind"
6"	8"	10"
Escorts	Gigolos	Hustlers
The Bikini Brief	The G-String	The Full Monty

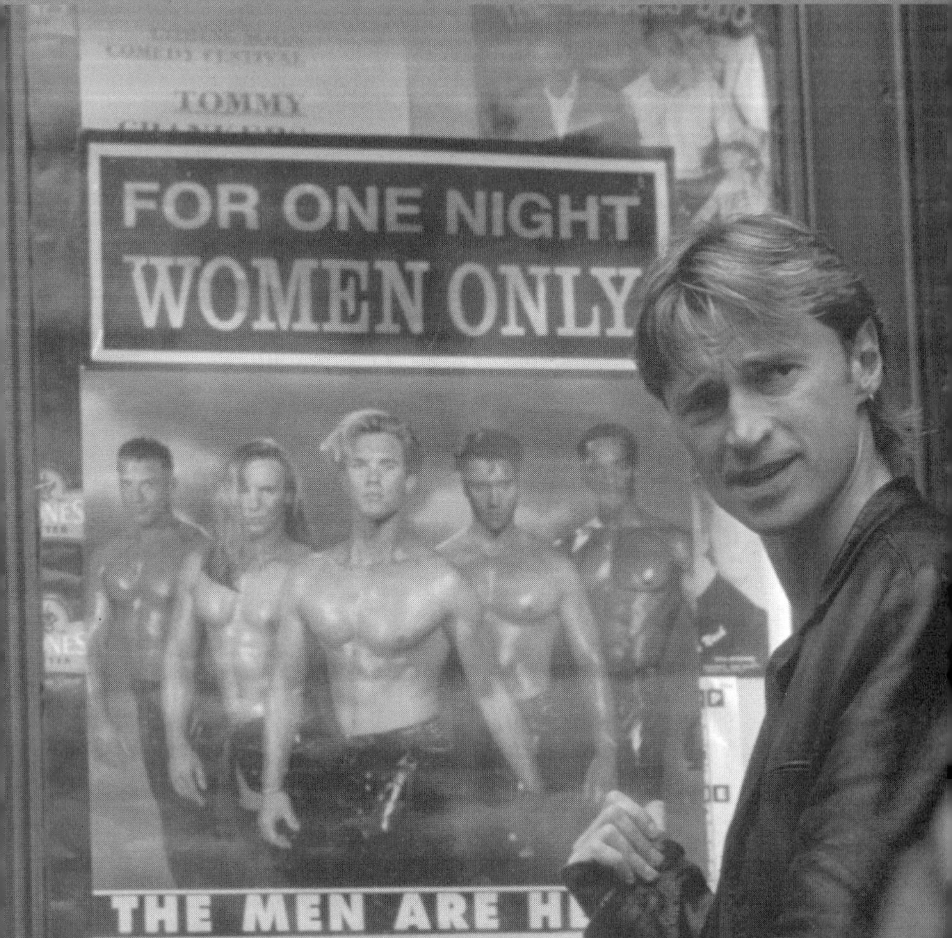
TOMMY
FOR ONE NIGHT
WOMEN ONLY
THE MEN ARE H
MAY 4TH • 7•00 p.m.

STUD PUPPET

Q&A

WITH A FULL MONTY MAN

Q: WHAT'S THE MOST IMPORTANT ASSET TO A MALE STRIPPER?
A: Believe it or not, I would say muscle flexibility and agility. Muscles and all that isn't as important as being able to do some really nasty bends and deep grinds. When women go to see a male stripper, they want to see his body do things they don't normally see. It's not just about dancing.

Q: I DON'T HAVE MUCH BELOW THE WAIST, BUT THE REST OF ME LOOKS PRETTY GOOD—SHOULD I GO THE FULL MONTY?
A: It depends how small you're talking. You'll find women are very forgiving when it comes your size if you've given them a good time with your dance. If you're abnormally small, you may want to keep a little something on—always best to leave them wanting more.

Q: I HAVE TERRIBLE BUNIONS AND PRETTY BAD HAMMER TOES. WOMEN ALWAYS COMMENT ON HOW UGLY MY FEET ARE. CAN I KEEP MY SHOES ON DURING A STRIPTEASE?
A: Absolutely! Most guys do. Shoes are hard to get off when your dancing anyway—if you're going to wear shoes, construction boots look hot.

Q: I'VE NOTICED THAT MOST MALE STRIPPERS HAVE NO HAIR ON THEIR CHESTS, AND I DO. SHOULD I SHAVE IT?

A: The reason most strippers shave their chests is because it makes the pecs look more cut. Same with the legs, you can see the calf muscles better. Some guys look better with hair if they don't have big pecs; the hair will disguise you.

Q: HOW REHEARSED SHOULD A STRIPTEASE BE?
A: Some dance troops do totally rehearsed shows with little or no audience interaction. But if you know your music really well, you can improvise because you'll know what's coming next and how much time you've got. It's not important to have every move down.

Q: WHAT KIND OF MUSIC IS BEST TO STRIP TO?
A: Anything with a steady dance beat. An extended mix is better though, since most songs only last about three minutes and you won't even get your shirt unbuttoned in three minutes.

Q: I DON'T HAVE THE GREATEST BODY, BUT I'M A GREAT DANCER. HOW IMPORTANT IS IT FOR A STRIPPER TO HAVE A GREAT BODY?
A: If you're going pro, very important. But if your working small bars or parties, a sense of fun will make up for what you body lacks.

The Ten Most Common Misconceptions about Male Strippers

THE NAKED TRUTH

1) All male strippers are gay.
While there certainly are gay strippers working the "for women only" circuit, there *is* such a thing as a heterosexual male stripper—but you might be hard-pressed to find one.

2) Male strippers get their tan lines from natural exposure to the sun.
We don't believe this phenomenon *has ever* occurred. We assert that 100% of male exotic dancers are card-carrying members of a private tanning salon.

3) Their hair always looks like that.
Yes and no. It *does* always look like that, but only because they spend a king's ransom—as well as hours in the bathroom—to ensure that it does.

4) They all have big penises.
For the most part, this is absolutely false. Important to take into consideration: If a man is compelled to spend that much time at a gym, on a tanning bed, and in a hair salon, he's obviously over-compensating for *something*.

5) All male strippers are single.
Not true. Believe it or not, there are some women who have said "I do" to a man who earns his living taking his clothes off for large groups of strange—and most often drunk—women.

6) They'd never really take it *all* off.
Hardly. Many male strippers have appeared in hard-core photo layouts and adult videos. Think twice before you give an exotic dancer a good-natured smooch—you never know where those lips have been!

7) Male strippers have naturally hairless chests, legs, and backs.
Few men do. For the male stripper, shaving doesn't end with the face. In fact, many strippers opt for rigorous and costly depilatory treatments to maintain that satiny-smooth sheen.

8) Male strippers eat right and exercise.
Exercise is certainly important for the professional stripper; washboard abs and chiseled pecks are money in the bank. While some do it the hard way, others prefer steroids. And for some, cocaine and ecstasy are favored over wheatgrass juice and protein powder.

9) They're all gigolos.
Not all, but pretty damn close. Everyone has their price, especially a male exotic dancer.

10) All male strippers are self-obsessed and extremely vain.
Just wanted to see if you were paying attention—this one's absolutely true. All male strippers *are* completely self-obsessed, no question there!

Gender Gripes:

For decades women have complained that men have it too easy. Sure, women are the ones who bear children, bear a monthly attack of PMS, and bear the media-induced pressure to fight the aging process with a never-ending series of diets, beauty aids, and plastic surgery. But open your eyes and look around you—who do you really think has it easier, someone like Cher or someone like Burt Reynolds? Liz Taylor or George Hamilton? Farrah Fawcett or Jan-Michael Vincent? Certainly both sides look pretty grim. The fact of the matter is that men have had just as tough a time as women, but not until recently did they have a forum through an ever-growing number of Fitness, Health, and Fashion magazines in which to complain about it.

When you take a cold, hard look, it would seem that both mother nature *and* modern culture are as equally cruel to males as they are to females.

Here's our proof:

FOR WHOM IS LIFE THE TOUGHEST?

Female trouble

Crows feet

Cutting yourself while shaving

Trimming fat off the thighs

Sexual harassment on the job

The high cost of breast implants

Cellulite

6'2" with heels

Panty hose

Marrying rich

A fat ass

Trying hard to live up to the standards set by swimsuit ads

Menopause

Hot flashes

Waxing unwanted hair from your bikini line

A pap smear

Sagging breasts

Phen-Fen

The ticking of your biological clock

Maladies for men

Hair loss

Cutting yourself while shaving

Deflating the spare tire

No action on the weekends

The high cost of penis enlargement

Ear hair

5'6" with lifts

Neckties

Marrying someone young enough to be your daughter

A flat ass

Trying hard to live up to the standards set by underwear ads

Mid-life crisis

Erectile dysfunction

Waxing unwanted hair from your back

A prostate exam

Sagging breasts

Rogaine

The insurance payments on your foreign sports car

MEN OBSESS ABOUT THEIR BODIES TOO!!

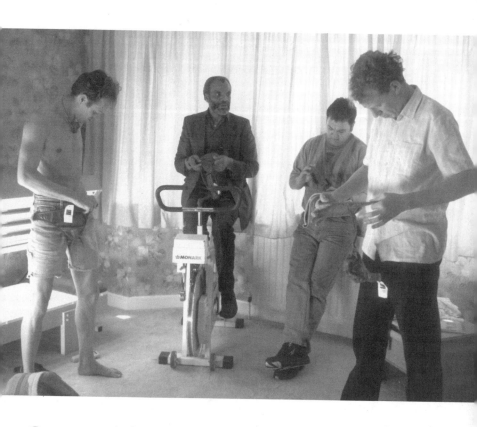

Q: HOW WOULD YOU CHANGE YOUR BODY IF YOU HAD A MAGIC WAND??

We asked

Dan, 40, High School Teacher
Mike, 35, Computer Programmer
Jason, 25, Student
Jim, 42, C.P.A.
Richard, 37, Bookstore Manager
Stephan, 34, Photographer
Chuck, 31, Social Worker

And they said:

Dan: If I had a magic wand, I'd add some inches below the waist; I'm just average. I went bald in my twenties, and as much as I'd like to have hair again, if I had to choose between having a full head of hair, or another inch on my dick, I'd choose the extra inch.

Mike: I'd want a flatter stomach and no spare tire. Whenever I gain weight, it goes straight to my gut, and if I don't want to gain weight I have to watch everything I eat, *everything*. I have friends who can eat whatever they want and they never gain an ounce; it's totally unfair. My body will stabilize at about fifteen to twenty pounds over my ideal weight and stay there, but to go any lower than that I have to put myself on a strict diet and exercise like a fiend. I wish I had a high metabolism and could eat whatever I wanted and still stay thin—I don't even care about muscles. I hate the term "love handles" and I hate it when my wife grabs my fat.

Jason: My arms are like broomsticks—all my life people have made fun of my skinny arms. Even if I work with weights, my arms get muscle definition, but stay thin and boney. My elbows are so sharp and pointy they could kill. Thank god that the junkie-look became hip, so being skinny is somewhat fashionable.

Jim: My feet are almost totally flat. The main problem with this is that I break in shoes in a really weird way. Shoes never look right on me, and I can't wear really soft shoes because my feet just smash them down all around and flatten them like a pancake. Hush Puppies have become so popular, but I can't wear them because the body of the shoe is too soft and my foot would crush the arches right down to the ground. Whenever I see men with bare feet, I always turn green with envy when I spot a set of strong, high arches.

Dan: My butt is flat as a board, and kind of wide, and it looks like a woman's butt. There are no exercises to fix this.

Richard: It's disgusting, and I'm embarrassed to admit this, but I still get pimples on my back. I don't know why god has cursed me with this terrible condition—maybe I was a real bastard in a past life and this is my karmic debt. It's terrible, and I know it's a total turn-off to women.

Stephan: I'm way too hairy, and it doesn't seem to stop growing. I have hair growing in places now where I didn't have hair five years ago and it's frightening. I keep wondering where I'll have hair ten years from now. I feel like I should start socking money away for electrolysis treatments.

Chuck: My hair started falling out about six years ago, and I'll probably have a shiny head before I hit forty. I really don't care about losing my hair because it never, *ever* looked good when I had it. I don't think I ever in my life experienced a "good hair day." And now, I save hundreds of dollars a year on haircuts,

which is good. In a way, losing my hair makes me feel liberated, but whenever I run into someone I haven't seen in ten years or more, in spite of the fact that I look good in every other respect—I haven't gotten fat or anything—I know the first thing they think is "Oh my gosh, *he went bald!*" Your baldness precedes you. So I wish I had hair just on those occasions.

Jim: I'd like to have some hair on my chest, just a little. I'm 42 and when I take off my shirt I look like a 12 year old.

Richard: About the time I hit 35, my body began to sag in places that it never did before, and that was kind of weird. Places that I never even considered now look a little weathered. But I'm not going to waste my life in a gym because it's all going to sag anyway sooner or later, but if I had a magic wand that's what I'd change—but I'm not fanatical about it.

You too can have

A STRIPPER'S

TAN LINE

IN 15 MINUTES!

Using The Full Monty Insta-tan Method in the privacy of your own home!!!

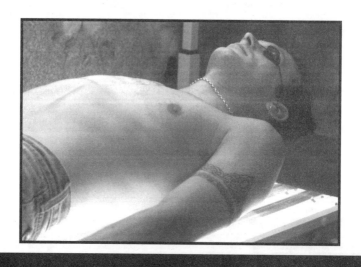

When male stripping hit big during the 80s an interesting aesthetic emerged along with it: The stripper tan line.

The stripper tan line doesn't happen by due process or by accident like a farmer's tan. A stripper tan line is a high-contrast, deliberate, carefully maintained affectation, and is as much a part of the stripper's costume—or lack of it—as his G-string. A defined tan line gives that *nuder-than-naked* look to a stud puppet for whom nothing comes between his sun-scorched epidermis and his squealing audience. And for many, that sharp band of contrasting skin tone wrapping around the tight waist and firm buttocks of a male exotic dancer is nothing less than a super-charged aphrodisiac!

While the professional might have hours to spend "sunning" in a tanning booth or roasting by the pool—the laymen may not. What if you're an amateur with a real job and a busy schedule that doesn't allow room for such lollygagging? And why spend all that time in the sun when you take into consideration the long-term damage from those merciless UVA/UVB rays?

Good news: you're not out of luck. You can have that nuder-than-naked look too—*and in only fifteen minutes!* Just follow *The Full Monty Insta-tan Method!* Here's how:

What you will need:

-One can of temporary spray-on hair color, matched to one shade darker than your natural skin tone (available at any beauty supply shop).
-One pair of snug fitting bikini briefs (Note: the skimpier the better, as this will be the template for your tan line).
-A household electric fan.

Instructions:

Remove all your clothes except for the bikini briefs. Hold the can of spray color (shake well) approximately twelve to fifteen inches from the area of your waist and upper thighs, and lightly spray in a swift, broad, sweeping movement from right to

left. Move clockwise around your waist (being sure to get the insides of your thighs and buttocks) until you get a light and evenly applied "skin tone." Once you have finished, *be careful not to touch any part of the sprayed area!*

Next, stand in front of the electric fan (on high), alternating your body from front to back, allowing the spray to dry completely, about four minutes. If a darker tan line is desired, reapply another layer of spray. Once dry, carefully remove the bikini briefs, doing your best not to smear your "tan," and discard. Now carefully slip on your G-string.

The Full Monty Insta-tan Method is best applied ten to fifteen minutes prior to performing. If possible, maintain room temperature at 65 degrees or cooler, since your "tan" will loosen, streak, and run down your legs if you work up a sweat.

Precautionary Statements:

The Full Monty Insta-tan Method is harmful if swallowed. Do not inhale spray mist. Not recommended for strippers with chronic respiratory problems such as asthma, emphysema, or obstructive lung disease. Avoid contact with eyes. Do not use or mix with other quick-tanning products. Keep out of reach of children. If skin irritation develops, consult a physician.

NEVER WATUSI WITH A BEER GUT

THE BEST MOVES FOR YOUR BODY TYPE!

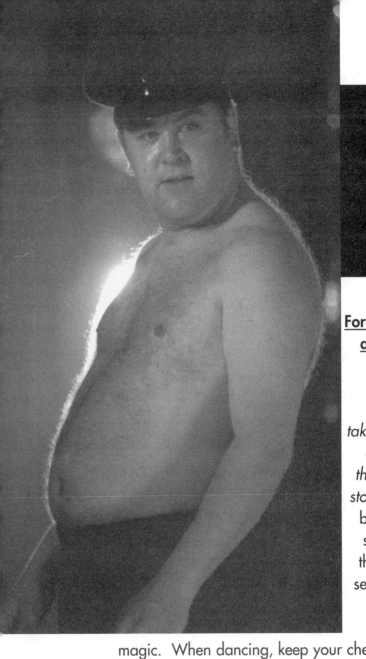

For beer bellies and Buddha-like guts:

You want to *take advantage of the moves that flatten the stomach.* Back bends (with a short stool or the cushioned seat of a chair for support) work like magic. When dancing, keep your chest up, shoulders back, spine arched, and arms outstretched high. NO FORWARD BENDS! DO NOT GET ON ALL FOURS! AVOID LAP DANCES! Move slowly, work the arms, neck, and head.

For the skin-and-bones stripper:

Don't jump around too fast or you'll look like a grasshopper. Stick with steady, hard moves like "The Jerk" or the "Surfer Stomp." Lean back and kneel

down for some pelvic thrusts to accentuate the stomach muscles. Do the "Body Wave" in a push-up position to show off the muscles in the arms and shoulders. Try the "bun shake." Don't flail the arms.

For medium to husky builds:

Work the quicker dances, concentrating your movement in the knees and upper thighs. Work the arms. Do the "Floor Hump" with your back arched. While standing, lean back and thrust the pelvis; keep arms and shoulders back to accentuate the chest. Try military style push-ups, clapping in time with the music. With a medium build, you can get away with a lot of hip movement. Turn your back and do some writhing forward bends—nasty!

DANCE BOY, DANCE!

A look at the dance crazes that rock our world

THE TWIST

Chubby Checker, King of the Twist, says: "It's like putting out a cigarette with both feet and coming out of a shower and wiping your bottom with a towel to the beat of the music—it's just that simple."

The Twist hit big in the early sixties, and was considered such a brazenly shocking display of raw sex that it was denounced by communists, and banned at school functions across the U.S.. The Twist was one of the first popular dances where partners danced apart, not together. The craze caught like wildfire, mostly because of it's sexual overtones, but also because even a dork with two left feet could manage an effective Twist.

Twistin' Tunes:
The Twist, Chubby Checker
Twistin' the Night Away, Sam Cook
Peppermint Twist, Chubby Checker
Twist and Shout, The Beatles
Ultra Twist, The Cramps

THE HUSTLE

What do you think of when you think of the Hustle; design[er] jeans? Famolares? Curling irons? Qiana photoprint shirt[s?] Feathered hair? Wide ties and big lapels? Bonnie Bell lip gloss?

A repetitive, easy series of moves geared mostly for peop[le] who couldn't dance, popular only because it had an accompanyin[g] song by the same name.

Groovy songs to Hustle by:
The Hustle, Van McCoy
Shadow Dancing, Andy Gibb
(That's the Way) I Like It, K.C. and the Sunshine Band
Night Fever, The Bee Gees
More Than a Woman, Tavares

THE MACARENA

Sort of a Mexican Hokey Pokey. It's The Hustle of the 90s: Se[e] above.

Do The Macarena to:
The Macarena, Los Del Rio
(The list stops there because you'll look like an even bigger id[iot] doing the Macarena to any other song.)

BREAK DANCING

Overnight, it seemed that break dancing was everywhere in the 80s. But break dancers never limited their work to a dance floor like normal people. Busy urban sidewalks and over-populated beach promenades set the scene for the break dancer—always doing his thing on a large sheet of old cardboard, accompanied by a big and very loud *ghetto blaster*. Crowds would gather in amazement at the sight of a break dancer's high-speed seizure of spinning, *breaking*, *popping*, and *locking*, marveling at this demanding—and seemingly dangerous—new dance form. The break dancer's audience was often so appreciative that they would toss money into a donation cup, which the break dancer undoubtedly spent on chiropractic adjustments.

Fortunately, break dancing vanished from the urban scene as quickly as it appeared.

Try *Breakin'* it to the sounds of:
Rapper's Delight, Sugar Hill Gang
That's the Joint, Funky Four + 1
The Adventures of Grand Master Flash and the Wheels of Steel, Grand Master Flash & The Furious Five
Break Dancin'/Electric Boogie, West Street Mob
White Lines (Don't Do It), Grand Master Flash & Melle Mel

THE FULL MONTY

Haven't seen this one yet? You will. Though the moves might seem a bit dodgy, it's a brilliant dance if you've got the hump. Some say you've got to be a nutter to give The Full Monty a try, what with takin' your kit off and puttin' the lunchbox on display. But you can't give a toss what your mates might think—if your Full Monty isn't a cockup, you just might have a queue of birds waiting to stuff brass in your kegs—and we're not kidding! A brill dance for reet horny lassies on a wild night out.

The Full Monty is more brazen than The Twist, more studied than The Hustle or The Macarena, and gathers an even bigger crowd than a Break Dance. Talented feet and a sense of rhythm are not as important to The Full Monty as courage; the moves are easy, but the dance is nothing without 100% follow-through. Security guard uniforms can be used if you're going for complete authenticity, but are not necessary—breakaway trousers, however, are. Work your necktie and your belt, each one separately and slowly. Keep hold of your hat.

You can improvise your way through a routine with a series of standard F.M. moves. Slow thrusting from the groin is a popular one, as is the isolated and steady forward shimmy of the shoulders (in time with the music). As a variation on the shoulder shimmy, place your arms akimbo and try it again—feel like a bloody fool? Then you're doing it right!

Always take your kit off in the following order, making no exceptions: 1) The tie. 2) The belt. 3) The shirt. 4) The pants (breakaway; otherwise reverse #s 4 & 5). 5) The shoes (optional) 6) The rest. But work the hat, and work the hat again, before flinging it like a Frisbee. Note: It's very difficult to remove your shoes and socks and still look sexy.

Go The Full Monty to:
You Sexy Thing, Hot Chocolate
You Can Leave Your Hat On, Tom Jones
Hot Stuff, Donna Summer
I Touch Myself, Divinyls
Je T'aime Moi Non Plus, Serge Gainsbourg and Jane Birkin
The Stripper, Joe Loss and His Orchestra

THE
FULL
MONTY
SLANG
DICTIONARY

WHAT THE HELL ARE THEY REALLY SAYING?

all in, exhausted, **I'm all in** = *Gosh, I'm beat!*

all to cock, screwed up, **cockup** = fuckup, botched

Arsenal, London soccer team

Barclaycard, a credit card issued by Barclays bank

beggar, a guy, **beggar** = dude; *you lucky beggar!*

bender, a male homosexual

benny, an outburst of anger, **to get a benny on** = to have a cow

blimey, an exclamation of surprise or annoyance [an abbreviated variation of *God blind me!*]

bloke, informal word for man

bloody, an intensifier, **you bloody fool!** = *you fucking asshole!*

bob, an informal word for a shilling, a coin

Bobby Charlton, soccer player

bog, bathroom, john

bog-eyes, a person screwing something up

bollocks, 1. a taboo word for balls [as in testicles] 2. an exclamation of annoyance or disbelief 3. bullshit, nonsense 4. **bollocksed,** and exclamation of hateful rage, or against another person or thing **bollocksed** = *damn you!/damn it!*

Bonfire Night, a British pyromaniac free-for-all similar in spirit to July 4th in the U.S.

bonnet, the hood of a car

brass, dough, bread, money

bugger, 1. A person who practices buggery 2. a taboo word for something or someone considered to be an asshole 3. a humorous or affectionate term for a man or a child, **bugger** = rascal 4. an exclamation of annoyance or disappointment **bugger!** = *shit!*

cheeky, snotty, impudent

chuffer, a wretched, vile individual

chuffing, a "polite" word for fucking

clock, to recognize

dick, 1. a guy 2. a taboo work for penis 3. **dickhead,** a taboo word for someone who's a total fucking moron, an absolute complete fucking idiot

divvy, oddball

dodgy, risky, uncertain, tricky

dole, an unemployment check 2. **on the dole,** on unemployment

effort, event, occasion

eppy, 1. an epileptic 2. to throw an eppy, to throw a fit

footy, football/soccer

full monty, the works, the whole enchilada 2. **to go the full monty** = to go all the way

git, a contemptible person, a fool

give over, = *are you shittin' me?*

glass paper, sand paper

grand, a thousand pounds

High Street, the main street of a town

holiday, vacation

hump, 1. to pout, to sulk 2. **to get the hump on,** to be in a fit of sulking

Job Club, similar to the unemployment office

jumble, junk donated to a jumble sale; **jumble sale** = rummage sale

kegs, pants

kit, 1. clothes, shoes, everything you're wearing 2. **to take my kit off** = to get naked

knockers, female breasts

lam, lamming, lammed, to whip, pummel, or beat

lunchbox, a guy's dick and balls

mate, pal

me, my

mug, 1. a person's face or mouth 2. a pushover, someone easily swindled

nowt as queer as folk, an adage meaning *there's is nothing more strange than people*

nutter, a kook

offside, 1. an illegal position in soccer 2. **offside trap,** a move forcing members of the opposite team to be offside

poof, poofter, a fairy, a male homosexual

posh, elegant, fashionable, top drawer, ritzy [supposedly an acronym of port out, starboard home: the most desirable locations for a cabin in British ships sailing to and from the East, being the shaded sides]

punter, 1. generally anyone, an average joe on the street 2. a customer, especially the customer of a hooker, a john

queue, a line of people or cars waiting to move forward

quid, slang word for pound, buck = dollar/quid = pound

reck, short for reckon

redundant, to lose your job because it's no longer necessary

reet, right

shag, shagging, shagged, fuck, fucking, fucked 2. to be exhausted, as in *I just flew in from London and boy, are my arms shagged!*

shag bucket, a person who's a big pain in the ass

sledging, sledge = sled, to travel across snow by sled

sodding, a strong exclamation of annoyance

sommut, something

squaddies, soldiers, members of the military squad

stripe me, an expression of surprise, irritation 2. **stripe,** a stroke of a whip, rod, cane

ta, thanks

tackle, cock and balls

tell what for, to tell someone off, to scold, to reprimand

Torvil, female member of the Torvil and Dean figure skating team

toss, 1. concern 2. **to not give a toss,** to not give a shit

tosser, a bum, a useless, worthless person

widger, penis

willy, penis

woofter, a male homosexual